God's Little Wonders

Simple Joys Through the Eyes of a Child

ARTWORK BY

Sandra Kuck

HARVEST HOUSE PUBLISHERS
Eugene, Oregon

God's Little Wonders

Copyright © 2002 by Harvest House Publishers
Eugene, Oregon 97402

ISBN 0-7369-0829-3

Design and production by Garborg Design Works, Minneapolis, Minnesota

Harvest House Publishers has made every effort to trace the ownership of all poems and quotes. In the event of a question arising from the use of a poem or quote, we regret any error made and will be pleased to make the necessary correction in future editions of this book.

Scripture quotations are taken from the Holy Bible, New International Version®, Copyright © 1973, 1978, 1984 by the International Bible Society. Used by permission of Zondervan Publishing House. The "NIV" and "New International Version" trademarks are registered in the United States Patent and Trademark Office by International Bible Society.

Printed in Hong Kong

02 03 04 05 06 07 08 09 10 11 / NG / 10 9 8 7 6 5 4 3 2 1

There is the unrestricted and full joy of a child's laughter, uncluttered by the worries of the rest of the world just affirming the pure unbridled joy of discovering God's world—sharing that joy through their laughter.

GERALD BRIAN THOMAS

Children are a wonderful gift… They have an extraordinary capacity to see into the heart of things.

DESMOND TUTU

In summer I am very glad
We children are so small,
For we can see a thousand things
That men can't see at all.

LAURENCE ALMA-TADEMA

TWINKLE

Twinkle, twinkle, little star,
How I wonder what you are!
Up above the world so high,
Like a diamond in the sky.

In the dark-blue sky you keep,
And often through my curtain peep,
For you never shut your eye
Till the sun is in the sky.

As your bright and tiny spark
Lights the traveler in the dark,
Though I know not what you are,
Twinkle, twinkle, little star.

JANE TAYLOR

STAR

The  Swing

How do you like to go up in a swing,
  Up in the air so blue?
Oh, I do think it the pleasant thing
  Ever a child can do!

Up in the air and over the wall,
  Till I can see so wide,
Rivers and trees and cattle and all
  Over the countryside—

Till I look down on the garden green;
  Down on the roof so brown—
Up in the air I go flying again,
  Up in the air and down!

ROBERT LOUIS STEVENSON

They are idols of hearts and of households;
they are angels of God in disguise;
The sunlight still sleeps in their tresses,
His glory still gleams in their eyes...

CHARLES M. DICKINSON

He called a little child and had him stand among them.
And he said: "I tell you the truth, unless you change and become
like little children, you will never enter the kingdom of heaven.
Therefore, whoever humbles himself like this child is the greatest
in the kingdom of heaven. And whoever welcomes a little child
like this in my name welcomes me."

THE BOOK OF MATTHEW

I see the Moon,
And the Moon sees me;
God bless the Moon,
And God bless me.

CELTIC RHYME

A Boy's Song

Where the pools are bright and deep,

Where the gray trout lies asleep,

Up the river, and over the lea,

That's the way for Billy and me.

Where the blackbird sings the latest,

Where the hawthorne blooms the sweetest,

Where the nestlings chirp and flee,

That's the way for Billy and me.

Where the mowers mow the cleanest,

Where the hay lies thick and greenest;

There to trace the homeward bee,

That's the way for Billy and me.

Where the hazel bank is steepest,

Where the shadow falls the deepest,

Where the clustering nuts fall free,

That's the way for Billy and me.

JAMES HOGG

Sandra Kuck

Sea Shell, Sea Shell,
  Sing me a song, O please!
A song of ships, and sailor men,
  And parrots, and tropical trees,

Of islands lost in the Spanish Main
  Which no man ever may find again,
Of fishes and corals under the waves,
  And sea horses stabled in great green caves.

Sea Shell, Sea Shell,
  Sing of the things you know so well.

AMY LOWELL

Education commences at the mother's knee, and every word spoken within the hearing of little children tends towards the formation of character.

HOSEA BALLOU

God sends children for another purpose than merely to keep up the race—to enlarge our hearts; and to make us unselfish and full of kindly sympathies and affection; to give our souls higher aims; to call out all our faculties to extended enterprise and exertion and to bring round our firesides bright faces, happy smiles, and loving, tender hearts. My soul blesses the great Father, every day, that he has gladdened the earth with little children.

MARY HOWITT

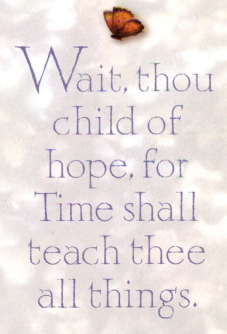

Oh that it were my chief delight
To do the things I ought!
Then let me try with all my might
To mind what I am taught.

ANN TAYLOR

Wait, thou
child of
hope, for
Time shall
teach thee
all things.

MARTIN FARQUHAR TUPPER

"Would you tell me, please, which way
     I ought to go from here?"
"That depends a good deal on where
     you want to get to," said the Cat.
"I don't much care where—" said Alice.
"Then it doesn't matter which way you go,"
     said the Cat.
"—so long as I get somewhere," Alice added
     as an explanation.
"Oh, you're sure to do that," said the Cat,
     "if you only walk long enough."

LEWIS CARROLL
ALICE IN WONDERLAND

The children bring us laughter,
and the children bring us tears;
They string our joys, like jewels
bright, upon the thread of years;
In every place where humans toil,
in every dream and plan,
The laughter of the
children shapes the
destiny of man.

EDGAR A. GUEST

I think when I read that sweet story of old,

When Jesus was here among men,

How he called little children as lambs to His fold,

I should like to have been with them then.

I wish that His hands had been placed on my head,

That His arm had been thrown around me,

And that I might have seen His kind look when He said,

"Let the little ones come unto me."

JEMIMA LUKE

Children are the hands by

which we take hold of heaven.

*C*hildren live in a world directed by the senses as animals seem to do, and when the two meet, there arises an immediate bond, providing a sense of security, of pleasure, and of quiet understanding… Animals teach children friendship and loyalty, gentleness and kindness, and responsibility, too. They teach about birth and death and about the precious life to be experienced in between.

PAMELA PRINCE
"THE BEST OF FRIENDS"

Children make your life important.

ERMA BOMBECK

Out came the children running.

All the little boys and girls,

With rosy cheeks and flaxen curls,

And sparkling eyes and teeth like pearls,

Tripping and skipping, ran merrily after

The wonderful music with shouting and laughter.

ROBERT BROWNING
"THE PIED PIPER"

It is [children] who
are God's presence,
promise and hope
for mankind.

MARIAN WRIGHT EDELMAN

There was once a child, and he strolled about a good deal, and thought of a number of things. He had a sister, who was a child, too, and his constant companion. These two used to wonder all day long. They wondered at the beauty of the flowers; they wondered at the height and blueness of the sky; they wondered at the depth of the bright water; they wondered at the goodness and the power of God who made the lovely world...

There was one clear shining star that used to come out in the sky before the rest, near the church spire, above the graves. It was larger and more beautiful, they thought, than all others, and every night they watched for it, standing hand in hand at the window. Whoever saw it first, cried out, "I see the star!" And often they cried out both together, knowing so well when it would rise, and where. So they grew to be such friends with it, that before lying down in their beds, they always looked out once again, to bid it good night; and when they were turning around to sleep, they used to say, "God bless the star!"

CHARLES DICKENS
"A CHILD'S DREAM OF A STAR"

Children's voices
Between the

For a child watching through a hole in the fence above the yard, it is a wonder world of mystery and movement. The child loves all the noise, and then it loves the silence of the wind that comes before the full rush of the pounding train, that bursts out from the tunnel where it lost itself and all its noise in darkness, and the child loves all the smoke, that sometimes comes in rings, and always puffs with fire and blue color.

GERTRUDE STEIN

in the orchard blossom - and the fruit-time:

T.S. ELIOT

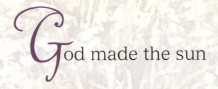

God made the sun

And God made the tree,

God made the mountains

And God made me.

"I thank you, O God,

For the sun and the tree

For making the mountains

And for making me."

LEA GALE

The potential possibilities of any child are the most intriguing and stimulating in all creation.

RAY L. WILBUR

You cannot catch a child's spirit by running after it; you must stand still and for love it will soon itself return.

ARTHUR MILLER

I am the Child.
All the world waits for my coming.
All the earth watches with interest
　　to see what I shall become.
Civilization hangs in the balance.
For what I am, the world of
　　tomorrow will be.

I am the Child.
I have come into your world,
　　about which I know nothing.
Why I came I know not;
How I came I know not.
I am curious; I am interested.
I am the Child.
You hold in your hand my destiny.
You determine, largely, whether
　　I shall succeed or fail.

MAMIE GENE COLE

In the tall grass they lay still as mice and watched flocks of little prairie chickens running and pecking around their anxiously clucking, smooth brown mothers. They watched striped snakes rippling between the grass stems or lying so still that only their tiny flickering tongues and glittering eyes showed that they were alive…And sometimes there'd be a great gray rabbit, so still in the lights and shadows of a grass clump that you were near enough to touch him before you saw him…His nose wiggled, and sunlight was rosy through his long ears, that had delicate veins in them and the softest short fur on their outsides. The rest of his fur was so thick and soft that at last you couldn't help trying, very carefully, to touch it.

LAURA INGALLS WILDER
LITTLE HOUSE ON THE PRAIRIE

There is always one moment in childhood when the door opens and lets the future in.

GRAHAM GREENE

Behold, children are a gift of the Lord.

THE BOOK OF PSALMS

The Tide

Sometimes we peep beneath the blinds
And through the window bars,
We see the dew like silver clouds:
We see the lighted stars.

And down among the sea-weed pools
Where little fishes hide,
Swift coming through the dark we hear
The footsteps of the tide.

We know, when night is tucked away,
To-morrow there will be
Across the flat and shining sand
The footprints of the sea.

MARJORIE WILSON

And so the time passed happily on till evening. Then the wind began to roar louder than ever through the old fir trees; Heidi listened with delight to the sound, and it filled her heart so full of gladness that she skipped and danced round the old trees, as if some unheard of joy came to her.

JOHANNA SPYRI
HEIDI

Grant, we beseech thee, O heavenly Father, that the child of this thy servant may daily increase in wisdom and stature, and grow in thy love and service, until he come to thy eternal joy; through Jesus Christ our Lord. Amen.

THE BOOK OF COMMON PRAYER

Anne knelt at Marilla's knee and looked up gravely.

"Why must people kneel down to pray? If I really wanted to pray I'll tell you what I'd do. I'd go out into a great big field all alone or into the deep, deep woods, and I'd look up into the sky—up- up- up- into that lovely blue sky that looks as if there was no end to its blueness. And then I'd just feel a prayer…"

L.M. MONTGOMERY
ANNE OF GREEN GABLES

You're special and different, it clearly appears.

Not one other person has your eyes and ears.

God made all your fingers, your nose, and your hair.

You're our special blessing, an answer to prayer.

We're glad that God made you, our dearest and Best!

Let's thank God together, then lie down to rest.

HELEN HAIDLE

Soft is
the
heart
of a
child.
Do not
harden
it.

AUTHOR
UNKNOWN

The children bring us laughter, and the children bring us tears; They string our joys, like jewels bright, upon the thread of years; They bring the bitterest cares we know, their mother's sharpest pain, Then smile our world to loveliness, like sunshine after rain.

EDGAR GUEST

Children are likely to live up to what you believe in them.

LADYBIRD JOHNSON

*Train a child in
the way he should
go, and when he is
old he will not
turn from it.*

THE BOOK OF PROVERBS

Behold the child,
by nature's kindly law
Pleased with a rattle,
tickled with a straw.

ALEXANDER POPE

Children
have neither
a past nor
future; they
rejoice in
the present.

LA BRUYÈRE

*C*hildren are made of eyes and ears, and nothing, however minute, escapes their microscopic observation.

FANNY KEMBLE

How beautiful is youth! How bright it gleams

With its illusions, aspirations, dreams!

Book of Beginnings, Story without End,

Each maid a heroine, and each man a friend!

HENRY WADSWORTH LONGFELLOW

The greatest poem ever known

Is one all poets have outgrown:

The poetry, innate, untold,

Of being only four years old.

CHRISTOPHER MORLEY

45

Paper Boats

DAY by day I float my paper boats one by one down the
running stream.

In big black letters I write my name on them and the
name of the village where I live.

I hope that someone in some strange land will find them
and know who I am.

I load my little boats with *shiuli* flowers from our garden,
and hope that these blooms of the dawn will be
carried safely to land in the night.

I launch my paper boats and look up into the sky and see
the little clouds setting their white bulging sails.

I know not what playmate of mine in the sky sends
them down the air to race with my boats!

When night comes I bury my face in my arms and dream
that my paper boats float on and on under
the midnight stars.

RABINDRANATH TAGORE

When little Elizabeth whispers
  Her morning-love to me,
Each word of the little lisper's,
  As she clambers on my knee—
Hugs me and whispers, "Mommy,
  Oh, I'm so glad it's day
And the night's all gone away!"
How it does thrill and awe me,—
  "The night's all gone away!"

"Sometimes I wake all listenin',"
  She sighs, "and all's so still!—
The moon and the stars half-glistenin'
  Over the window-sill;
And I look where the gas's pale light
  Is all turned down the hall—
And you ain't here at all!—
And oh! how I wish it was daylight!
  —And you ain't here at all!"

JAMES WHITCOMB RILEY

47

Children make
a special kind
of sense all
their own.

ART LINKLETTER